Zane Hogan
101 Fishing Jokes
© 2017, Zane Hogan

Self-published
All rights reserved.

zanehoganbooks@gmail.com

101 FISHING JOKES

BY: ZANE HOGAN

What is a fisherman's favorite game show?

Name That Tuna.

What's the best way to catch a fish?

Have someone throw it at you.

George went fishing, but at the end of the day he had not caught one fish. On the way back to camp, he stopped at a fish store. I want to buy three trout, he said to the owner.

But instead of putting them in a bag, throw them to me. "Why should I do that?" the owner asked. So I can tell everyone that I caught three fish!

Where does a fisherman get his hair cut?

The bobber shop.

I just swallowed
a fish bone!

You must be
choking.

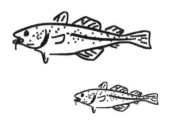

Without a
trout.

Did you hear about the fish whose left side was cut off?

He's all right now.

Why did Batman
stop bringing
Robin to go
fishing?

He kept
eating all
the worms.

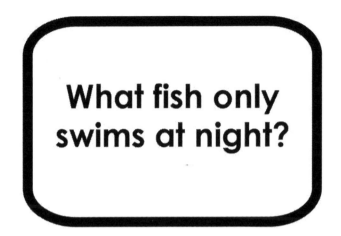

What fish only swims at night?

A starfish.

Why did the angler get a job at the sardine factory?

Because of his can do attitude.

Why did the
young man go
fishing?

To find a
gillfriend.

Why should you use six hooks on your fishing line?

Efishancy.

What do romantic fish sing to each other?

Salmon-chanted evening.

What did the fish say when he hit the concrete wall?

Dam.

Did you hear
about the fish
who were suing
the fisherman?

It's a bass
action suit.

Cook a man a fish and you feed him for a day.

Teach a man to fish and you can get rid of him for the whole weekend.

Two parrots are sitting on a perch.

The first one says to the other, "Do you smell fish?"

What birthday party game do fish like to play?

Salmon Says.

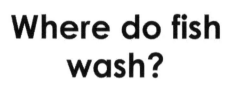

Where do fish
wash?

In a river
basin.

How do fish
keep up with
what's
happening in
the world?

Current
news.

What did the fishing mathematician eat for lunch?

Fish pi.

Why was the whistling fisherman angry?

Because he was always out of tuna.

Rules:
1. Bait your own hook.
2. Clean your own fish.

3. Tell your own lies.

Where do fish keep their money?

A riverbank.

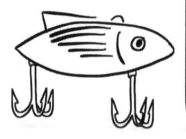

Where do fish get their cool clothes?

Abercrombie and Fish.

Did you hear about the paddle sale at the boat shop?

It was quite the oar deal.

What keeps a fish singing his best?

Autotuna.

Why are fish so gullible?

They fall for things hook, line and sinker!

What happens when you put nutella on salmon?

You get salmonella.

What's a knight's favorite fish?

Swordfish.

What fish likes to make you an offer you can't refuse?

The Codfather.

What do you call
a dangerous fish
that drinks too
much ?

A beer-a-
cuda !

What fish do you want to have in the operating room?

A sturgeon.

What kind of money do fishermen make?

Net profits.

How do
shellfish get to
the hospital?

In a clam-
bulance.

Why did Pythagoras win the fishing competition?

Everyone knows he's a good angler.

What kind of
fish will help
you hear
better?

A herring
aid!

A pet store
had a fishing
contest.

No perches
necessary.

Where do fish go on holiday?

Finland.

Who is a fisherman's favorite author?

Salmon Rushdie.

My dad likes to cook his fish with butter, milk and cream.

How dairy!

What is the best kind of music to listen to when fishing?

Something catchy.

What did the magician say to the fisherman?

Pick a cod, any cod!

What do naked
fish play with?

Bare-a-
cudas.

Why did the musician keep on fishing?

He was waiting for a bass soon.

The trout attacked the perch with a skeleton.

But fish that live in bass houses shouldn't throw bones.

How do you communicate with a fish?

Drop it a line.

Where do shellfish go to borrow money?

The prawn broker.

What do you call a man with a large flatfish on his head?

Ray.

Give a Nigerian a fish and he'll eat for a day.

Teach a Nigerian to phish, and he'll immediately turn into a prince and try to scam you.

My father and I went fishing.

When he caught a small shark, he called it his dadliest catch.

What did the pope have for lunch?

Holy mackerel.

Why was the angler bad at boxing?

He only threw hooks.

What does a bunny use when it goes fishing?

A harenet.

Which fish dresses the best?

The swordfish, it always looks sharp.

What was the
humpback's
favorite TV
show?

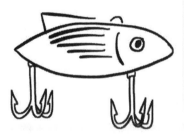

Whale of
Fortune.

Why do fish swim in schools?

Because they like taking debate.

What does a ladies man like to fish with?

Allure.

Two fish are sitting
in a tank.
One looks over at
the other and
says,

"Hey, do
you know
how to
drive this
thing?"

How do the fish get to school?

Octo-bus.

What fish make the best sandwich?

A peanut butter and jellyfish.

Why did the
fish blush?

Because
he saw the
boat's
bottom.

Work...

that annoying time between fishing trips.

How many fishermen does it take to change a light bulb?

One, but you should have seen the bulb, it was THIS big.

I only fish with earthworms.

Well, what other planet would they be from?

Give a man a fish and feed him for a day.

Teach a man to fish and he will sit in a boat and drink beer all day.

Two guys rented a fishing boat, and were having a great day catching fish. The first guy says, "This is such a great spot, we need to mark it so we can come back." The second guy proceeded to put a mark on the side of the boat.

The first guy asks "What are you doing?" The second guy replies, "Marking the spot." "Don't be stupid," the first guy says, "what if we don't get the same boat next time?"

What do you get if you cross a trout with an apartment in Europe?

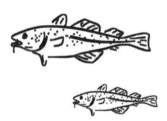

A flat fish.

Why is it easy to weigh a fish?

Because they have built-in scales.

One day a confused ice fisherman drilled a hole into the ice and peered into it. A loud voice said, "There are no fish down there." He walked several yards away and drilled another hole and peered into that hole and again the voice said, "There are no fish down there."

He then walked about 50 yards away and drilled another hole and again the voice said, "There are no fish down there." He looked up into the sky and asked, "God, is that you?" "No, you idiot," the voice said, "it's the rink manager."

What's another name for a pirate ship?

A thug boat.

What do you
call a girl who
catches fish?

Annette.

Did you hear why the cops were called down to the seafood restaurant?

Two fish got battered.

How do you send a fish to your friend in another state?

You send it COD or first bass mail.

A guy calls his boss and says "I can't come to work today." The boss asks why and the guy says, "It's my eyes."

"What's wrong with your eyes?" asks the boss. "I just can't see myself coming to work, so I'm going fishing instead."

What do you call a Sith Lord who likes to fish?

Darth Wader.

What's a fish's favorite 80s song?

"I'll Stop the World and Smelt With You."

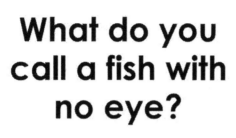

What do you
call a fish with
no eye?

Fsh.

What is an eel's favorite dance?

The electric slide.

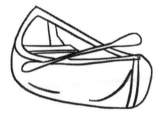

Why did the fish get embarrassed?

The sea weed.

One day, two guys Tom and Bob were out fishing. A funeral service passes over the bridge they're fishing by, and Bob takes off his hat and puts it over his heart. He does this until the funeral service passes by.

Tom then says, "Gee Bob, that was respectful of you!" Bob then replies, "It's the least I could do. After all I was married to her for 30 years."

Have you ever hunted bear?

No, but I've been fishing in my underwear.

How did the angler feel after repairing his net?

Mesh better, thanks.

Have you seen the new fishing website?

It went on line yesterday.

What is Putin's favorite fish?

Tsardines.

What's the difference between a fishing senior and a high school senior?

One baits his hooks while the other hates his books.

How many anglers does it take to change a light bulb?

Four. One to change the light bulb and three to brag about the one that they would have changed, but it got away.

What's a British cannibal's favorite meal?

Fish and chaps.

I caught a twenty pound salmon last week. Were there any witnesses?

There sure were. If there hadn't been, it would have been forty pounds.

Heard the one about the three guys that went ice fishing and didn't catch anything?

By the time they cut a hole big enough for the boat to fit into, it was time to go home.

Two fishermen were out on the lake when one of them dropped his wallet. As they watched the wallet float down to the depths of the lake, a carp came along and snatched up the wallet.

Soon came another carp who stole it away and then a third joined in. Remarked one of the fisherman, "That's the first time I've ever seen carp-to-carp walleting.

A priest was walking along the beach when he came upon two locals pulling another man ashore on the end of a rope. "That's what I like to see," said the priest, "a man helping his fellow man."

As he was walking away, one local remarked to the other, "Well, he sure doesn't know the first thing about shark fishing."

What happened when the two worms met in the on hook?

It was larva at first sight.

If you can
think of a
better fish pun,

let
minnow.

Printed in Great Britain
by Amazon

33279117R00061